Poetry for Young People

Robert Browning

Edited by Eileen Gillooly
Illustrated by Joel Spector

Sterling Publishing Company, Inc.
New York

For Jake, Kate, and particularly for Ben
and his invaluable assistance.

—Eileen

To my Princess Rowena, my muse.
And my Pixies: Max, Ari, Jacob & Saskia.

—Joel

Library of Congress Cataloging-in-Publication Data

Browning, Robert, 1812-1889.
[Poems. Selections]
Robert Browning / edited by Eileen Gillooly ; illustrated by Joel Spector.
p.   cm.— (Poetry for Young People)
Includes index.
ISBN 0-8069-5543-0
1. Children's poetry, English. [1. English poetry.] I. Gillooly, Eileen.
II. Spector, Joel. III. Title IV. Series
PR4203.G55 2000
821'8—dc2   00–058317

2   4   6   8   10 9   7   5   3

Grateful acknowledgment is made to Armstrong Browning Library, Baylor University,
Waco, Texas, to reproduce the 1837 drawing of Robert Browning
by Amédée de Ripert-Monclar found on page 4.

Published by Sterling Publishing Co., Inc.
387 Park Avenue South, New York, N.Y. 10016
Text © 2001 by Eileen Gillooly
Illustrations © 2001 by Joel Spector
Distributed in Canada by Sterling Publishing
c/o Canadian Manda Group, One Atlantic Avenue, Suite 105
Toronto, Ontario, Canada M6K 3E7
Distributed in Great Britain by Chris Lloyd at Orca Book Services,
Stanley House, Fleets Lane, Poole BH15 3AJ England
Distributed in Australia by Capricorn Link (Australia) Pty. Ltd.
P.O. Box 704, Windsor, NSW 2756, Australia

Printed in China

Sterling ISBN 0-8069-5543-0

Contents

INTRODUCTION
"I give you the truth broken into prismatic hues."

Robert Browning is one of the most beloved English poets—and one of the most difficult to read. Even his wife, the poet Elizabeth Barrett Browning, found his work hard to understand at times, and she often urged him to express himself more directly. His friend Thomas Carlyle, another famous writer of the 1800s, commented that for Browning "the problem of all problems" was clarity. And an early reviewer called his verses "somewhat mystical, somewhat poetical, somewhat sensual, and not a little unintelligible."

The poems in this volume are some of Browning's most "reader-friendly," but even these require quite a few definitions and explanations. One reason for this is that Browning was an enthusiastic reader on all kinds of subjects, and he poured his wide and varied knowledge into his poetry. As a result, the people and places he talked about were often unknown to his audience. This is especially true of the earlier poems. Both "Boot and Saddle" (page 15) and "Incident of the French Camp" (pages 18–19) require some knowledge of history to appreciate them fully. But once we understand this, most of Browning's poems open up to us without too much trouble. For Browning is actually less interested in the historical events than in the psychology of his speakers—how they think and feel and what motivates them to act. Two of his favorite themes are the eternal mystery of the human heart and the sometimes great and surprising difference between what we expect in life and what actually happens. "I give you the truth broken into prismatic hues," he told Elizabeth, by which he meant that truth is generally seen not as whole and absolute, but separated into bits and pieces, the way a prism separates colors. Truth, he believed, looks quite different from different perspectives. What seems true to his speaker may not seem at all true to the listener. "My Last Duchess" (pages 20–22) illustrates this irony brilliantly. The Duke's speech reveals something about his character that he does not recognize in himself—or would not want to reveal if he did.

"All my writings are purely dramatic," Browning once claimed, whether they were actual plays written for the stage, verse dramas like *Pippa Passes* (see page 9), story poems like "Echetlos" (pages 42–43), or dramatic monologues like "After" (page 24) or "My Last Duchess." In a dramatic monologue, the poet takes on the character and psychology of another person, the same way an actor does in a play. And, typically, the identity of a Browning speaker is as rich and complex as any character in drama or fiction. His goal was to portray "Action in Character, rather than Character in Action," to dramatize the thoughts and feelings of his speakers, rather than their physical actions. He wanted to reveal their inner struggles and moral conflicts, to chart what he called the "development of the soul." To do this, he needed to arouse the senses of his readers, to have them see and hear his speakers vividly, in the same way that they might view a painting or listen to a piece of music. Some of his poems, in fact, appeal mostly to the ear and are more like musical verses than poems, such as "Through the Metidja to Abd-el-kadr" (pages 16–17). Others, like the haunting "Love among the Ruins" (pages 30–32), conjure up both a picture and a melody with equal force. All of his poems, though, are intended to make us think. Browning believed that poets should instruct their readers as well entertain them. Throughout his life, his goal was to write poetry that would help people to understand themselves and their world.

Robert Browning was born on May 7, 1812—the third Robert Browning in three generations—in the small village of Camberwell, a suburb of London. His grandfather Robert Browning was a successful businessman who had inherited through his wife a financial interest in a slave plantation in the West Indies. When Browning's father was a young man, his grandfather sent him to the plantation to oversee the family's investments. Robert II was so sickened by the treatment of the slaves there that he refused to do what his father had ordered and returned to England instead. Grandfather Browning was enraged by his son's disobedience and refused to speak to him for many years.

Browning's father was a scholar, as Browning tells us in "Development" (pages 38–39), a poem in which he thanks his father for shaping his early education so wisely. Although Robert II worked as a clerk for the Bank of London, his real interests were books, paintings, and music. He was a *bibliophile*—a lover of books—and collected them with a passion. In fact, the cottage in which young Robert grew up was entirely lined with books—more than 6,000 of them. Browning was encouraged by his father to explore the huge family library, and many of his poems show the influence of his wide-ranging reading. He could read and write by the time he was five years old, and he was even younger when he began impressing his parents and their friends with the rhymes he composed. His family was a close-knit one, and Browning and his sister, Sarianna, and their parents lived a quiet and contented life together.

Most of Browning's education took place at home. As a young child, he attended a neighborhood school for a short time, but apparently was so much more knowledgeable and quick-witted than his classmates that the other children's parents complained, and he was asked to leave. Like most other middle-class English boys in the early 1800s, Browning was sent away to school at the age of eight. He declared later in life that he had learned nothing there. When he was fourteen years old, he returned to Camberwell to study under his father's direction. At home, his father taught him Latin and Greek and arranged for tutors in art, music, French, German, and Italian. Browning excelled in all these subjects. If you look closely, you can detect his love for them in his poetry. In "Old Pictures in Florence" (pages 26–27), for example, he tries to "paint" the Italian landscape in words. Both Browning's parents took great pride in his quick intelligence and artistic talents. Given their own personal beliefs, they were also surprisingly patient with him when he became an atheist and a vegetarian, for a time, in honor of the Romantic poet Percy Bysshe Shelley, whose work he greatly admired.

In 1828, Browning was sixteen years old and ready to go off to college. Brought up by his mother as a member of a Protestant Calvinist church, Browning was not permitted to attend college at Oxford or Cambridge, because they required all students to pledge an oath of allegiance to the Church of England. Realizing the trouble his son would have getting a good university education elsewhere, Browning's father became a founding member of the University of London, which had no religious requirements. Browning was the sixteenth student to enroll at the new university. He dropped out, however, after only a few months and returned home, where he continued to educate himself in his father's library, preparing himself to be a poet and working on getting his parents to agree to it. It's not easy to make a living as a poet, as his parents knew, and his mother was especially worried about his future. Nevertheless, they solidly supported him— both emotionally and financially—in his efforts to make poetry his career. His father, in fact, paid the production costs of many of his early books.

His first volume of poetry, entitled *Pauline, A Fragment of a Confession*, was published when Browning was just 21 years old. Although it received strong praise from some reviewers, not a single copy was sold. The plays he wrote, mostly for the great Victorian actor William Macready, were also unsuccessful. None of them ran for more than a handful of performances. Such disappointments, however, had little effect on Browning's cheerful, confident sense of well-being and purpose. He knew that his writing called upon his readers to ponder his meaning more than other poets' work did, and that many would give up before they understood him. Full of good will and easy conversation, Browning enjoyed meeting people and was an extremely popular dinner guest at the homes of other writers and artists. There he met all the literary celebrities of his day, including the poet William Wordsworth and the novelist George Eliot. Some people called Browning the greatest "diner out" in all of London.

By the time Browning was thirty years old, his poetry had earned him the respect of other writers and thinkers, though it was still not popular with the general public. In 1842 the most accomplished and highly admired female poet of the day, Elizabeth Barrett, referred to Browning in an article she wrote. She said he was a young poet of great potential, certain to be—along with Alfred Lord Tennyson—a leading voice of his generation. Although Browning had not yet met Miss Barrett, he was grateful to her for her good opinion, and he wrote her a letter to tell her so—though it took him nearly three years to do it! In it, he eagerly returned her admiration: "I love your verse with all my heart, dear Miss Barrett . . . and I love you too." In this way began one of the most famous romances of the century.

As in every great love story, there were obstacles to be overcome. Elizabeth was the oldest of twelve children, and her father forbade any of them to marry. Those who did were disowned. In addition, Elizabeth was an invalid and rarely left her bed, suffering from headaches, insomnia, chest pains, and fainting spells. The windows of her bedroom were sealed shut for more than half the year and were so heavily shaded that she never saw daylight. It took Browning many months to get her permission to visit, and another year to persuade her to marry him. Knowing that her father would do everything in his power to prevent their marriage, they eloped to Italy. She was 40 years old; Browning was 34. Although they occasionally visited England, France, and other parts of Italy, Florence quickly became their home, where they lived until Elizabeth's death in 1861. It was there, in 1849, that their only child, Robert Wiedemann Barrett Browning (nick-named "Pen"), was born. During these years in Italy, Browning published one of his most impor-tant collections of poetry, *Men and Women*, but he devoted the greater part of his time and energy to caring for his wife. Upon Elizabeth's death in 1861, he returned to London, where he lived for another 28 years. When Browning's father died in 1866, his sister Sarianna joined him and took charge of his household. He never remarried.

Although Browning's best known poems were published in the 1840s and 1850s, he contin-ued to write poetry until the end of his life. Despite Elizabeth's advice to strive for greater clar-ity, his poems seemed as baffling as ever to many readers in the 1880s. By then, literary societies had sprung up all over England to study the works of the country's greatest writers, such as Chaucer and Shakespeare. Much to Browning's embarrassment, the Browning Society—founded in 1881—became the first of its kind dedicated to studying the works of a living writer. The members of the Society hoped to figure out Browning's deep but often obscure thought by puz-zling over his poems together. In America, the interest in Browning and his work became a craze. His books began selling in record numbers, and even Midwestern train routes were named after his poems: *Pauline*, *Paracelsus*, and *Sordello*. American Browning Society members actually wore brown as they pored over his poems, sitting in rooms decorated in brown, and eating brown bread off brown plates! Browning Societies exist even today, though their obsession with the color brown seems to have vanished.

Until just a few months before he died, Browning's life was full of energy and spirit. He would wake up early, play the piano, visit art galleries, and go for walks with friends. He accepted almost as many invitations to dinner parties at the age of 75 as he had fifty years earlier. His weekends were packed with visitors, including American tourists who would stop by unexpectedly to question him about his poetry, which annoyed his sister. On a trip to Italy to visit his son Pen, Browning's health began to fail rapidly. His last book of poems, entitled *Asolando* (the Prologue appears on page 41), was published on December 12, 1889—the very day he died. He lived long enough, however, to learn that the book had been well reviewed and almost every copy had been sold. He was 77 years old. Pen accompanied his father's body back to England for the funeral. Browning is buried in Poets' Corner in Westminster Abbey next to Alfred Lord Tennyson.

PIPPA'S SONG

*These lines come from
Browning's verse play* Pippa
Passes, *which is one of the ear-
liest and most admired of his
long poems. The words "God's in
his heaven——/All's right with
the world!" are among the most
famous in English poetry.*

The year's at the spring
And day's at the morn;
Morning's at seven;
The hill-side's dew-pearled;
The lark's on the wing;
The snail's on the thorn:
God's in his heaven—
All's right with the world!

THE PIED PIPER OF HAMELIN: A CHILD'S STORY

When Browning was a young boy, his father told him the German folktale of the Pied Piper. Many years later, he wrote his own version as a get-well present for the son of the actor William Macready. The poem has been edited to fit the space in this book and still give you a sense of the story. Each cut is indicated by an ellipsis, or series of three dots (...).

. . . Rats!
They fought the dogs and killed the cats,
   And bit the babies in the cradles,
And ate the cheeses out of the vats,
   And licked the soup from the cooks' own
     ladles,
Split open the keys of salted sprats,
Made nests inside men's Sunday hats,
And even spoiled the women's chats,
   By drowning their speaking
   With shrieking and squeaking
In fifty different sharps and flats.

At last the people in a body
   To the Town Hall came flocking: . . .

An hour they sat in council
   At length the Mayor broke silence: . . .
"Oh for a trap, a trap, a trap!"
Just as he said this, what should hap
At the chamber door but a gentle tap?
"Bless us," cried the Mayor, "what's that?" . . .
"Only a scraping of shoes on the mat?
Anything like the sound of a rat
Makes my heart go pit-a-pat!"

sprats—*herrings; a type of fish*

"Come in!"—the Mayor cried, looking bigger:
And in did come the strangest figure!
His queer long coat from heel to head
Was half of yellow and half of red,
And he himself was tall and thin,
With sharp blue eyes, each like a pin,
And light loose hair, yet swarthy skin,
No tuft on cheek nor beard on chin,
But lips where smiles went out and in. . . .

swarthy—*dark*

And, "Please your honours," said he, "I'm able,
By means of a secret charm, to draw
All creatures living beneath the sun,
That creep or swim or fly or run,
After me so as you never saw! . . .
If I can rid your town of rats
Will you give me a thousand guilders?"
"One? fifty thousand!" was the exclamation
Of the astonished Mayor and Corporation.

Into the street the Piper stept . . .
And ere three shrill notes the pipe uttered,
You heard as if an army muttered;
And the muttering grew to a grumbling;
And the grumbling grew to a mighty rumbling;

guilders—*gold coins*

And out of the houses the rats came tumbling. . . .
From street to street he piped advancing,
And step for step they followed dancing,
Until they came to the river Weser,
Wherein all plunged and perished! . . .

You should have heard the Hamelin people
Ringing the bells till they rocked the steeple.
"Go," cried the Mayor, "and get long poles!
Poke out the nests and block up the holes!
        . . . When suddenly, up the face
Of the Piper perked in the market-place,
With a, "First, if you please, my thousand
guilders!"

A thousand guilders! The Mayor looked blue;
So did the Corporation too. . . .
To pay this sum to a wandering fellow
With a gypsy coat of red and yellow!
"Beside," quoth the Mayor with a knowing wink,
"Our business was done at the river's brink;
We saw with our eyes the vermin sink,
And what's dead can't come to life, I think. . . .
Beside, our losses have made us thrifty.
A thousand guilders! Come, take fifty!"

The Piper's face fell, and he cried,
"No trifling! I can't wait, beside! . . .
And folks who put me in a passion
May find me pipe to another fashion." . . .

"You threaten us, fellow? Do your worst,
Blow your pipe there till you burst!"

vermin—obnoxious animals; here, the rats

Once more he stept into the street; . . .
    And ere he blew three notes . . .
There was a rustling that seemed like a bustling
Of merry crowds justling at pitching and hustling,
Small feet were pattering, wooden shoes clattering,
Little hands clapping and little tongues chattering,
And, like fowls in a farm-yard when barley is scattering,
Out came the children running.
All the little boys and girls,
With rosy cheeks and flaxen curls. . . .

. . . As they reached the mountain's side,
A wondrous portal opened wide,
As if a cavern was suddenly hollowed;
And the Piper advanced and the children followed,
And when all were in to the very last,
The door in the mountain-side shut fast.

BOOT AND SADDLE

Part III of the poem "Cavalier Tunes," "Boot and Saddle" is actually a song. A supporter of Charles I of England discovers that his castle is under attack by the troops of Charles's enemy Oliver Cromwell and gallops home. Notice how the chorus's only line—"Boot, saddle, to horse, and away!"—urges flight rather than rescue in the end, quite the opposite of what it meant in the first three stanzas.

I

Boot, saddle, to horse, and away!
Rescue my castle before the hot day
Brightens to blue from its silvery grey,
    CHORUS: *Boot, saddle, to horse, and away!*

II

Ride past the suburbs, asleep as you'd say;
Many's the friend there, will listen and pray
"God's luck to gallants that strike up the lay—
    CHORUS: *"Boot, saddle, to horse, and away!"*

III

Forty miles off, like a roebuck at bay,
Flouts Castle Brancepeth the Roundheads' array:
Who laughs, "Good fellows ere this, by my fay,
    CHORUS: *"Boot, saddle, to horse, and away!"*

IV

Who? My wife Gertrude; that, honest and gay,
Laughs when you talk of surrendering, "Nay!
I've better counsellors; what counsel they?
    CHORUS: *"Boot, saddle, to horse, and away!"*

gallants—*noblemen; followers of the king*
lay—*song*
roebuck—*a male deer*
flouts—*scoffs at or scorns*

Castle Brancepeth—*the speaker's home*
Roundheads—*nickname for the Puritans, followers of
    Cromwell, owing to their severely clipped hair*
fay—*faith*

THROUGH THE METIDJA TO ABD-EL-KADR

When he was 22, Browning traveled as a diplomatic secretary to Russia, where he spent many weeks galloping from city to city in a horse-drawn carriage. The rapid, constant movement of the horses sank deeply into his memory and imagination, as you can see in this poem about the Algerian struggle for independence.

I

As I ride, as I ride,
With a full heart for my guide,
So its tide rocks my side,
As I ride, as I ride,
That, as I were double-eyed,
He, in whom our Tribes confide,
Is descried, ways untried
As I ride, as I ride.

II

As I ride, as I ride
To our Chief and his Allied,
Who dares chide my heart's pride
As I ride, as I ride?
Or are witnesses denied—
Through the desert waste and wide
Do I glide unespied
As I ride, as I ride?

III

As I ride, as I ride,
When an inner voice has cried,
The sands slide, nor abide
(As I ride, as I ride)
O'er each visioned homicide
That came vaunting (has he lied?)
To reside—where he died,
As I ride, as I ride.

IV

As I ride, as I ride,
Ne'er has spur my swift horse plied,
Yet his hide, streaked and pied,
As I ride, as I ride,
Shows where sweat has sprung and dried,
—Zebra-footed, ostrich-thighed—
How has vied stride with stride
As I ride, as I ride!

V

As I ride, as I ride,
Could I loose what Fate has tied,
Ere I pried, she should hide
(As I ride, as I ride)
All that's meant me—satisfied
When the Prophet and the Bride
Stops veins I'd have subside
As I ride, as I ride!

Metidja—*desert in Algeria*
Abd-el-kadr—*Arabian leader who organized resistance against French colonial rule*
double-eyed—*using binoculars*
Tribes—*Arab peoples*
descried—*seen in the distance*
Chief and his Allied—*Abd-el-kadr and his followers*
chide—*scold or find fault with*
unespied—*unnoticed*
vaunting—*bragging*
plied—*used*
pied—*having patches of color, especially black and white*
vied—*competed*
the Prophet—*Muhammad, founder of Islam*
the Bride—*Aisha, a wife of Muhammad, in whose arms he died*
subside—*lessen in force or intensity*

INCIDENT OF THE FRENCH CAMP

Napoleon Bonaparte, the great French general, was defeated by the Duke of Wellington at Waterloo in 1815 and died in exile. A year after Napoleon's death in 1841, Browning published this poem about a much too young and very brave soldier who gives his life for Napoleon's cause.

I

You know, we French stormed Ratisbon:
　　A mile or so away
On a little mound, Napoleon
　　Stood on our storming-day;
With neck out-thrust, you fancy how,
　　Legs wide, arms locked behind,
As if to balance the prone brow
　　Oppressive with its mind.

II

Just as perhaps he mused "My plans
　　That soar, to earth may fall,
Let once my army-leader Lannes
　　Waver at yonder wall,"—
Out 'twixt the battery-smokes there flew
　　A rider, bound on bound
Full-galloping; nor bridle drew
　　Until he reached the mound.

III

Then off there flung in smiling joy,
　　And held himself erect
By just his horse's mane, a boy:
　　You hardly could suspect—
(So tight he kept his lips compressed,
　　Scarce any blood came through)
You looked twice ere you saw his breast
　　Was all but shot in two.

IV

"Well," cried he, "Emperor, by God's grace
　　We've got you Ratisbon!
The Marshal's in the market-place,
　　And you'll be there anon
To see your flag-bird flap his vans
　　Where I, to heart's desire,
Perched him!" The Chief's eye flashed; his plans
　　Soared up again like fire.

V

The Chief's eye flashed; but presently
　　Softened itself, as sheathes
A film the mother-eagle's eye
　　When her bruised eaglet breathes;
"You're wounded!" "Nay," the soldier's pride
　　Touched to the quick, he said:
"I'm killed, Sire!" And his Chief beside
　　Smiling the boy fell dead.

Ratisbon—*city on the Danube River, attacked by Napoleon
　in 1809*
prone—*sloping downward*
vans—*wings*

My Last Duchess

Browning's most widely known and admired poem, "My Last Duchess," is a wonderful example of the dramatic monologue, in which the speaker unintentionally reveals his true character. Here the wealthy, respected, recently widowed Duke shows himself to be a monster of selfishness, arrogance, greed, and quite likely a murderer besides.

Ferrara

That's my last Duchess painted on the wall,
Looking as if she were alive; I call
That piece a wonder, now: Frà Pandolf's hands
Worked busily a day, and there she stands.
Will't please you sit and look at her? I said
"Frà Pandolf" by design, for never read
Strangers like you that pictured countenance,
The depth and passion of its earnest glance,
But to myself they turned (since none puts by
The curtain I have drawn for you, but I)
And seemed as they would ask me, if they durst,
How such a glance came there; so, not the first
Are you to turn and ask thus. Sir, 'twas not
Her husband's presence only, called that spot
Of joy into the Duchess' cheek: perhaps
Frà Pandolf chanced to say "Her mantle laps
Over my lady's wrist too much," or "Paint
Must never hope to reproduce the faint
Half-flush that dies along her throat;" such stuff
Was courtesy, she thought, and cause enough
For calling up that spot of joy. She had
A heart . . . how shall I say? . . . too soon made glad,
Too easily impressed; she liked whate'er
She looked on, and her looks went everywhere.
Sir, 'twas all one! My favour at her breast,
The dropping of the daylight in the West,
The bough of cherries some officious fool
Broke in the orchard for her, the white mule
She rode with round the terrace—all and each

Would draw from her alike the approving speech,
Or blush, at least. She thanked men,—good; but thanked
Somehow . . . I know not how . . . as if she ranked
My gift of a nine-hundred-years-old name
With anybody's gift. Who'd stoop to blame
This sort of trifling? Even had you skill
In speech—(which I have not)—to make your will
Quite clear to such an one, and say "Just this
Or that in you disgusts me; here you miss,
Or there exceed the mark"—and if she let
Herself be lessoned so, nor plainly set
Her wits to yours, forsooth, and made excuse,
—E'en then would be some stooping, and I choose
Never to stoop. Oh, Sir, she smiled, no doubt,
Whene'er I passed her; but who passed without
Much the same smile? This grew; I gave commands;
Then all smiles stopped together. There she stands
As if alive. Will't please you rise? We'll meet
The company below, then. I repeat,
The Count your Master's known munificence
Is ample warrant that no just pretence
Of mine for dowry will be disallowed;
Though his fair daughter's self, as I avowed
At starting, is my object. Nay, we'll go
Together down, Sir! Notice Neptune, though,
Taming a sea-horse, thought a rarity,
Which Claus of Innsbruck cast in bronze for me!

Ferrara—*town in northern Italy, ruled in the Renaissance by dukes*
    known for their cruelty
countenance—*expression of the face*
durst—*dared*
mantle—*long, loose robe or cloak-like garment*
officious—*meddlesome; offering unwanted help*
munificence—*generosity*
avowed—*admitted*

HOME-THOUGHTS, FROM ABROAD

In 1845, when this poem was published, Browning was planning to elope with Elizabeth Barrett to Italy. Although he enjoyed traveling and living abroad, he was sometimes homesick. Here Browning reminisces about springtime in England.

I

Oh, to be in England
Now that April's there,
And whoever wakes in England
Sees, some morning, unaware,
That the lowest boughs and the brushwood sheaf
Round the elm-tree bole are in tiny leaf,
While the chaffinch sings on the orchard bough
In England—now!

II

And after April, when May follows,
And the whitethroat builds, and all the swallows!
Hark, where my blossomed pear-tree in the hedge
Leans to the field and scatters on the clover
Blossoms and dewdrops—at the bent spray's edge—
That's the wise thrush; he sings each song twice over,
Lest you should think he never could recapture
The first fine careless rapture!
And though the fields look rough with hoary dew,
All will be gay when noontide wakes anew
The buttercups, the little children's dower
—Far brighter than this gaudy melon-flower!

sheaf—*bundle*
brushwood—*broken branches*
bole—*the base of a tree trunk*
chaffinch—*a type of finch or bird*
whitethroat—*a kind of sparrow or warbler*
rapture—*ecstatic joy; great delight*
hoary—*white with frost*
dower—*property*
gaudy—*tasteless and showy*

MY STAR

*The speaker loves his star not because of its greatness, but
because of the special relationship they share. Notice how the
form of the poem, too, is special. Rarely do lines lengthen as a
poem progresses, as they do here.*

All that I know
      Of a certain star
Is, it can throw
      (Like the angled spar)
Now a dart of red,
      Now a dart of blue;
Till my friends have said
      They would fain see, too,
My star that dartles the red and the blue!
Then it stops like a bird; like a flower, hangs furled:
   They must solace themselves with the Saturn above it.
What matter to me if their star is a world?
   Mine has opened its soul to me; therefore I love it.

angled—*faceted or having small
   polished plane surfaces
   (as on a cut gem)*
spar—*a kind of crystal*
fain—*gladly*
dartles—*makes darts out of*
furled—*rolled up*
solace—*console or comfort*

24

AFTER

The scene is the aftermath of a duel. Standing over the corpse of his rival, the victor feels avenged at first, but then wonders whether the death of his opponent has brought him any real satisfaction. By the end of the poem, he regrets his rashness and doubts the wisdom of settling conflicts by violence.

Take the cloak from his face, and at first
    Let the corpse do its worst.

How he lies in his rights of a man!
    Death has done all death can.

And, absorbed in the new life he leads,
    He recks not, he heeds
Nor his wrong nor my vengeance—both strike
    On his senses alike,
And are lost in the solemn and strange
    Surprise of the change.

Ha, what avails death to erase
    His offence, my disgrace?
I would we were boys as of old
    In the field, by the fold:
His outrage, God's patience, man's scorn
    Were so easily borne.

I stand here now, he lies in his place:
    Cover the face.

recks—*cares*
avails—*helps*

OLD PICTURES IN FLORENCE

*In these lines from the beginning of "Old Pictures in
Florence," Browning tries to paint the spirit of the
Italian landscape with words, conveying a sense of
the souls of things, places, and people.*

I

The morn when first it thunders in March,
    The eel in the pond gives a leap, they say:
As I leaned and looked over the aloed arch
    Of the villa-gate this warm March day,
No flash snapped, no dumb thunder rolled
    In the valley beneath where, white and wide
And washed by the morning water-gold,
    Florence lay out on the mountain-side.

II

River and bridge and street and square
    Lay mine, as much at my beck and call,
Through the live translucent bath of air,
    As the sights in a magic crystal ball. . . .

IV

On the arch where olives overhead
    Print the blue sky with twig and leaf,
(That sharp-curled leaf which they never shed)
    'Twixt the aloes, I used to lean in chief,
And mark through the winter afternoons,
    By a gift God grants me now and then,
In the mild decline of those suns like moons,
    Who walked in Florence, besides her men.

aloed—*covered with aloe, a kind of plant*
translucent—*permitting light to shine through; see*
    through, but misty

MEMORABILIA

*At the age of 14, Browning discovered the poetry
of Percy Bysshe Shelley and was "thunderstruck"
by it. Here, two poets share their memories of
Shelley: one who actually met him and the
other—the speaker—who was simply inspired by
him. The latter, like Browning himself, will
always remember the moor where he first read the
work of that eagle-eyed, far-seeing poet.*

I

Ah, did you once see Shelley plain,
  And did he stop and speak to you,
And did you speak to him again?
  How strange it seems, and new!

II

But you were living before that,
  And also you are living after,
And the memory I started at—
  My starting moves your laughter!

III

I crossed a moor, with a name of its own
  And a certain use in the world no doubt,
Yet a hand's-breadth of it shines alone
  'Mid the blank miles round about:

IV

For there I picked up on the heather
  And there I put inside my breast
A moulted feather, an eagle-feather—
  Well, I forget the rest.

*moor—large open tract of
  uncultivated land, with few
  shrubs*
*moulted—shed to make way
  for new growth*

MISCONCEPTIONS

Browning was often difficult to understand, but he could also write with great clarity, as he does in the first stanza of this poem. Like many of us at some point in life, the "spray" mistakes the bird's feelings towards it. It thinks the bird clings to it because she loves it— not, as we discover, because she plans to "use" it to build her nest.

This is a spray the Bird clung to,
    Making it blossom with pleasure,
Ere the high tree-top she sprung to,
    Fit for her nest and her treasure.
    Oh, what a hope beyond measure
Was the poor spray's, which the flying feet hung to,—
So to be singled out, built in, and sung to!

spray—*small branch bearing buds or flowers*

LOVE AMONG THE RUINS

Written on January 1, 1852, this poem looks to the past as well as to the future. It tells both of an ancient civilization wrecked by greed and war, and of the speaker's plans to meet his loved one among its ruins. Listen carefully, and you'll hear—in the short alternating lines of the stanzas reprinted here—an echo of that ruined past.

I

Where the quiet-coloured end of evening smiles
  Miles and miles
On the solitary pastures where our sheep
  Half-asleep
Tinkle homeward thro' the twilight, stray or stop
  As they crop—
Was the site of a city great and gay,
  (So they say)
Of our country's very capital, its prince
  Ages since
Held his court in, gathered councils, wielding far
  Peace or war.

II

Now,—the country does not even boast a tree,
  As you see,
To distinguish slopes of verdure, certain rills
  From the hills
Intersect and give a name to, (else they run
  Into one)
Where the domed and daring palace shot its spires
  Up like fires
O'er the hundred-gated circuit of a wall
  Bounding all,
Made of marble, men might march on nor be
   pressed,
  Twelve abreast.

crop—*eat off the tops of plants (as a sheep does grass)*
verdure—*fresh, green vegetation*
rills—*small brooks*
bounding—*forming the boundaries of*

V

And I know, while thus the quiet-coloured eve
  Smiles to leave
To their folding, all our many-tinkling fleece
  In such peace,
And the slopes and rills in undistinguished grey
  Melt away—
That a girl with eager eyes and yellow hair
  Waits me there
In the turret whence the charioteers caught soul
  For the goal,
When the king looked, where she looks now,
   breathless, dumb,
  Till I come.

folding—*coming together with a fenced enclosure or pen*
fleece—*sheep*
turret—*small ornamented tower*

VI

But he looked upon the city, every side,
    Far and wide,
All the mountains topped with temples, all the
        glades'
    Colonnades,
All the causeys, bridges, aqueducts,—and then,
    All the men!
When I do come, she will speak not, she will stand,
    Either hand
On my shoulder, give her eyes the first embrace
    Of my face,
Ere we rush, ere we extinguish sight and speech
    Each on each.

VII

In one year they sent a million fighters forth
    South and North,
And they built their gods a brazen pillar high
    As the sky,
Yet reserved a thousand chariots in full force—
    Gold, of course.
Oh heart! oh blood that freezes, blood that burns!
    Earth's returns
For whole centuries of folly, noise and sin!
    Shut them in,
With their triumphs and their glories and the rest!
    Love is best.

colonnades—*series of ordered columns*
causeys—*causeway, or a raised road across marshland or water*
aqueducts—*bridgelike structures designed to transport water*

RABBI BEN EZRA

In this famous first stanza of "Rabbi Ben Ezra," the Rabbi calls upon his listener to join him in celebrating old age, in embracing "the last of life" even more lovingly than "the first."

Grow old along with me!
The best is yet to be,
The last of life, for which the first was made:
Our times are in His hand
Who saith "A whole I planned,
Youth shows but half; trust God: see all,
     nor be afraid!"

FROM "JAMES LEE'S WIFE": IN THE DOORWAY

"James Lee's Wife" is a set of nine poems. "In the Doorway" is the third. Here Mrs. Lee urges her husband not to give way to depression or despair. Although the climate on the coast of Normandy is hostile and their fields are barren, their love ought to be strong enough for them to endure the hardships they face.

I

The swallow has set her six young on the rail,
      And looks sea-ward;
The water's in stripes like a snake, olive-pale
      To the leeward,—
On the weather-side, black, spotted white with the wind.
"Good fortune departs, and disaster's behind,"—
Hark, the wind with its wants and its infinite wail!

II

Our fig-tree, that leaned for the saltness, has furled
      Her five fingers,
Each leaf like a hand opened wide to the world
      Where there lingers
No glint of the gold, Summer sent for her sake:
How the vines writhe in rows, each impaled on its stake!
My heart shrivels up and my spirit shrinks curled.

III

Yet here are we two; we have love, house enough,
      With the field there,
This house of four rooms, that field red and rough,
      Though it yield there,
For the rabbit that robs, scarce a blade or a bent;
If a magpie alight now, it seems an event;
And they both will be gone at November's rebuff.

IV

But why must cold spread? but wherefore bring change
      To the spirit . . . ?
Oh, live and love worthily, bear and be bold! . . .

leeward—*the side toward which the wind blows*
furled—*rolled up*
impaled—*pierced with a sharp point*
rebuff—*sudden check (here by the weather) to
   progress or movement*

AMPHIBIAN

In these eight stanzas from "Amphibian," both the swimmer and the butterfly have escaped their earthbound lives for a time. Although the swimmer regrets that he cannot join the butterfly in its flight, he communes with it in spirit. The word amphibian literally means "living two ways."

1

The fancy I had to-day,
    Fancy which turned a fear!
I swam far out in the bay,
    Since waves laughed warm and clear.

2

I lay and looked at the sun,
    The noon-sun looked at me:
Between us two, no one
    Live creature, that I could see.

3

Yes! There came floating by
    Me, who lay floating too,
Such a strange butterfly!
    Creature as dear as new:

4

Because the membraned wings
    So wonderful, so wide,
So sun-suffused, were things
    Like soul and nought beside.

5

A handbreadth over head!
    All of the sea my own,
It owned the sky instead;
    Both of us were alone.

6

I never shall join its flight,
    For, nought buoys flesh in air.
If it touch the sea—good night!
    Death sure and swift waits there.

11

But sometimes when the weather
    Is blue, and warm waves tempt
To free oneself of tether,
    And try a life exempt

12

From worldly noise and dust,
    In the sphere which overbrims
With passion and thought,—why, just
    Unable to fly, one swims!

membraned—*tissue-like*
sun-suffused—*illuminated by the sun*
tether—*leash; a rope or chain restricting an*
    animal's movements

PISGAH-SIGHTS I

Like Moses, who looked down at the Promised Land from the top of Mt. Pisgah, the speaker in this poem has a God-like view of the world. He sees that life is always a balance of good and evil, joy and sorrow, "roughness and smoothness." The poem itself illustrates this balance in its halved lines and in the pairs of opposites that dominate these first three stanzas.

Over the ball of it,
   Peering and prying,
How I see all of it,
   Life there, outlying!
Roughness and smoothness,
   Shine and defilement,
Grace and uncouthness:
   One reconcilement.

Orbed as appointed,
   Sister with brother
Joins, ne'er disjointed
   One from the other.
All's lend-and-borrow;
   Good, see, wants, evil,
Joy demands sorrow,
   Angel weds devil!

"Which things must—*why* be?"
   Vain our endeavour!
So shall things aye be
   As they were ever.
"Such things should *so* be!"
   Sage our desistence!
Rough-smooth let globe be,
   Mixed—man's existence!

defilement—*pollution, filth*

orbed—*shaped into a sphere or circle*

desistence—*act of stopping to try*

DEVELOPMENT

Browning's father was his first and favorite teacher. He encouraged his son to use his imagination at a time when early education was largely a matter of memorizing. One of the few poems he composed without a rhyme scheme, this loving thank-you to his father was written at the end of Browning's life.

My Father was a scholar and knew Greek.
When I was five years old, I asked him once
"What do you read about?"
       "The siege of Troy."
"What is a siege and what is Troy?"
        Whereat
He piled up chairs and tables for a town,
Set me a-top for Priam, called our cat
—Helen, enticed away from home (he said)
By wicked Paris, who couched somewhere close
Under the footstool, being cowardly,
But whom—since she was worth the pains, poor puss—
Towzer and Tray,—our dogs, the Atreidai,—sought
By taking Troy to get possession of
—Always when great Achilles ceased to sulk,
(My pony in the stable)—forth would prance
And put to flight Hector—our page-boy's self.
This taught me who was who and what was what:
So far I rightly understood the case
At five years old: a huge delight it proved
And still proves—thanks to that instructor sage
My Father, who knew better than turn straight
Learning's full flare on weak-eyed ignorance,
Or, worse yet, leave weak eyes to grow sand-blind,
Content with darkness and vacuity.

Priam—*King of Troy and father of Paris and Hector*

Helen—*wife of Menelaus, kidnapped by Paris and taken to Troy*

Paris—*son of Priam, whose kidnapping of Helen started the Trojan War*

Atreidai—*sons of Atreus, Agamemnon and Menelaus*

Troy—*city in Asia Minor, destroyed by the Greeks in revenge for Paris's kidnapping of Helen*

Achilles—*the greatest Greek warrior*

Hector—*brother of Paris and the greatest Trojan warrior, killed by Achilles*

sand-blind—*half blind*

vacuity—*complete lack of ideas or emptiness of mind*

"Touch Him Ne'er So Lightly . . ."

Writing poetry is no easy task, as Browning knew from experience. Here he argues that poetry is less the product of inspiration than of long, persistent, and often fruitless labor. Even great poems—those that, like the pine tree, last from generation to generation—struggle to be born.

"Touch him ne'er so lightly, into song he broke:
Soil so quick-receptive,—not one feather-seed,
Not one flower-dust fell but straight its fall awoke
Vitalizing virtue: song would song succeed
Sudden as spontaneous—prove a poet-soul!"

                                     Indeed?
Rock's the song-soil rather, surface hard and bare:
Sun and dew their mildness, storm and frost their rage
Vainly both expend,—and few flowers awaken there:
Quiet in its cleft broods—what the after age
Knows and names a pine, a nation's heritage.

PROLOGUE TO *ASOLANDO*

These opening stanzas from the Prologue to Asolando *reflect on the change in a poet's concerns as he grows older. In his early years, a poet is likely to see himself in everything he looks at, or to cast the color of his own personality on what he sees. In old age, he tries to see the "very thing" itself, blazing forth through appearances or "outer seeming."*

"The Poet's age is sad: for why?
   In youth, the natural world could show
No common object but his eye
   At once involved with alien glow—
His own soul's iris-bow.

"And now a flower is just a flower:
   Man, bird, beast, are but beast, bird, man—
Simply themselves, uncinct by dower
   Of dyes which, when life's day began,
Round each in glory ran."

Friend, did you need an optic glass,
   Which were your choice? A lens to drape
In ruby, emerald, chrysopras,
   Each object—or reveal its shape
Clear outlined, past escape,

The naked very thing?—so clear
   That, when you had the chance to gaze,
You found its inmost self appear
   Through outer seeming—truth ablaze,
Not falsehood's fancy-haze?

iris-bow—*rainbow*
uncinct—*not surrounded*
dower—*gift*

optic—*pertaining to vision (i.e., eyeglasses)*
chrysopras—*a type of quartz*

ECHETLOS

The name "Echetlos" means "plowshare wielder" or one who fights with the cutting blade of a plow. Echetlos was a minor hero of the Battle of Marathon in 490 B.C., in which the Greeks successfully fought off the invading Persians. His actions were among the most famous of the battle, though his actual name was unknown. Browning suggests that our actions—not our names or looks or riches—are what truly earn us the respect of others. All but the last stanza of the poem is shown here.

Here is a story shall stir you! Stand up, Greeks dead and gone,
Who breasted, beat Barbarians, stemmed Persia rolling on,
Did the deed and saved the world, for the day was Marathon!

No man but did his manliest, kept rank and fought away
In his tribe and file: up, back, out, down—was the spear-arm play:
Like a wind-whipt branchy wood, all spear-arms a-swing that day!

But one man kept no rank and his sole arm plied no spear,
As a flashing came and went, and a form i' the van, the rear,
Brightened the battle up, for he blazed now there, now here.

Nor helmed nor shielded, he! but, a goat-skin all his wear,
Like a tiller of the soil, with a clown's limbs broad and bare,
Went he ploughing on and on: he pushed with a ploughman's share.

Did the weak mid-line give way, as tunnies on whom the shark
Precipitates his bulk? Did the right-wing halt when, stark
On his heap of slain lay stretched Kallimachos Polemarch?

Did the steady phalanx falter? To the rescue, at the need,
The clown was ploughing Persia, clearing Greek earth of weed,
As he routed through the Sakian and rooted up the Mede.

But the deed done, battle won—nowhere to be descried
On the meadow, by the stream, at the marsh,—look far and wide
From the foot of the mountain, no, to the last blood-plashed seaside,—

breasted—*confronted boldly*
stemmed—*stopped as if by damming*
rank—*standing side by side*
file—*standing one behind the other*
plied—*used*
van—*front*
helmed—*helmeted*
tiller—*one who prepares the soil for planting*
tunnies—*tuna*
precipitates—*throws or hurls downward*
Kallimachos Polemarch—*Athenian magistrate in charge of military affairs*
phalanx—*a formation of soldiers carrying overlapping shields and spears*
Sakian—*fighter on the side of the Persians*
Mede—*one who helped the Persians rule their empire*
descried—*seen in the distance*
blood-plashed—*lightly splashed with blood*

Not anywhere on view blazed the large limbs thonged and brown,
Shearing and clearing still with the share before which—down
To the dust went Persia's pomp, as he ploughed for Greece, that clown!

How spake the Oracle? "Care for no name at all!
Say but just this: 'We praise one helpful whom we call
The Holder of the Ploughshare.' The great deed ne'er grows small."

thonged—*crisscrossed with
narrow strips of leather*
shearing—*moving forward by
cutting away (as in shearing
wheat)*
Oracle—*the spokesperson for
the Greek god Apollo*

LA SAISIAZ

When Browning was in his late sixties, he visited a Swiss villa called La Saisiaz, where one of his traveling companions suddenly died. While the unusually short lines give a sense of how brief life is, Browning's tone in these opening stanzas is actually joyful. For death brings freedom from worry and care as well as the promise of eternal "sunshine and love."

I

Good, to forgive;
　Best, to forget!
　Living, we fret;
Dying, we live.
Fretless and free,
　Soul, clap thy pinion!
　Earth have dominion,
Body, o'er thee!

II

Wander at will,
　Day after day,—
　Wander away,
Wandering still—
Soul that canst soar!
　Body may slumber:
　Body shall cumber
Soul-flight no more.

III

Waft of soul's wing!
　What lies above?
　Sunshine and Love,
Skyblue and Spring!
Body hides—where?
　Ferns of all feather,
　Mosses and heather,
Yours be the care!

pinion—*the wing of a bird*
dominion—*rule, authority*

cumber—*weigh down or hinder*
waft—*act of floating gently through air*

PROLOGUE TO *DRAMATIC IDYLS*

Here, Browning finds it amusing that while people can't agree about what ails the body, they are nevertheless quick to prescribe for the ailing soul, about which they have even less understanding.

"You are sick, that's sure"—they say:
    "Sick of what?"—they disagree.
"'Tis the brain"—thinks Doctor A.,
    "'Tis the heart"—holds Doctor B.,
"The liver—my life I'd lay!"
    "The lungs!" "The lights!"
                Ah me!

So ignorant of man's whole
Of bodily organs plain to see—
So sage and certain, frank and free,
About what's under lock and key—
    Man's soul!

              lights—*eyes*

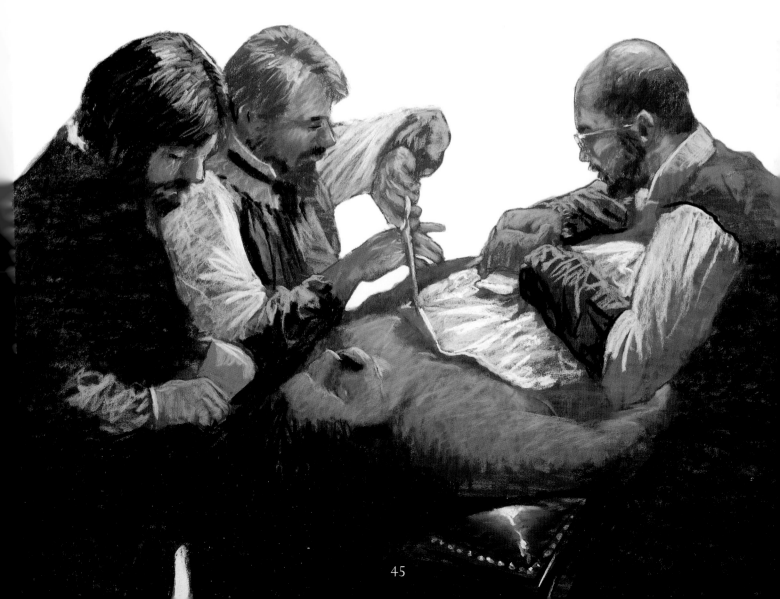

From "Jocoseria"

Without love, Browning declares, life is empty of meaning: a frame without a picture, beauty without a soul. This poem, of which a few lines are reprinted here, is a tribute of love to his wife written more than twenty years after her death.

Wanting is—what?
   Summer redundant,
   Blueness abundant,
   —Where is the blot?
Beamy the world, yet a blank all the same,
—Framework which waits for a picture to frame:
What of the leafage, what of the flower?
Roses embowering with nought they embower!
Come then, complete incompletion, O comer,
Pant through the blueness, perfect the summer!
   Breathe but one breath
   Rose-beauty above,
   And all that was death
   Grows life, grows love,
     Grows love!

Jocoseria—*a collection of humorous things*
wanting—*missing or lacking*
redundant—*more than what is needed*
beamy—*radiant or full of light*
embowering—*enclosing with a bower or frame
   providing leafy shelter*

PROSPICE

Perhaps the only thing we know for certain is that one day we will die. Although Browning acknowledges that death can be terrifying, he also looks forward to the last "fight" before eternal "peace." "Prospice" means "look forward" in Latin.

Fear death?—to feel the fog in my throat,
    The mist in my face,
When the snows begin, and the blasts denote
    I am nearing the place,
The power of the night, the press of the storm,
    The post of the foe;
Where he stands, the Arch Fear in a visible form,
    Yet the strong man must go:
For the journey is done and the summit attained,
    And the barriers fall,
Though a battle's to fight ere the guerdon be gained,
    The reward of it all.
I was ever a fighter, so—one fight more,
    The best and the last!
I would hate that death bandaged my eyes, and forbore,
    And bade me creep past.
No! let me taste the whole of it, fare like my peers
    The heroes of old,
Bear the brunt, in a minute pay glad life's arrears
    Of pain, darkness and cold.
For sudden the worst turns the best to the brave,
    The black minute's at end,
And the elements' rage, the fiend-voices that rave,
    Shall dwindle, shall blend,
Shall change, shall become first a peace, out of pain,
    Then a light, then thy breast,
O thou soul of my soul! I shall clasp thee again,
    And with God be the rest!

Arch Fear—*death*
summit—*highest point; top of a mountain*
guerdon—*reward*

forbore—*held back; refrained*
brunt—*main force or blow*
arrears—*overdue debt*

INDEX